The World and the Mysteries

by

Okito

A Once Upon a Bichon Publication
2017

Human Author: Esther Miller
Photography by Esther Miller and Larry Barnowsky
Book layout 2nd Edition: Larry Barnowsky

Email: transitions99@aol.com
Website: onceuponabichon.com

Print ISBN: 978-0-9764790-7-9
Digital ISBN: 978-0-9764790-8-6

This book is dedicated to Okito Barnowsky, a rare spirit in a dog body who brought joy to every person he met.

Printed in the United States of America by
Once Upon a Bichon
A division of Gyromagnetic Press
Cooperstown, NY

My name is Okito and this is a serious book.
It's about my world and some of the things I understand
and the other things, the things I don't understand.
I will call those things the "mysteries".

I have an outside world and

I have an inside world.

And I love both my worlds.

I am always trying to figure things out.

I watch everything very closely. Even if you don't see me I am probably still watching.

I watch from chairs.

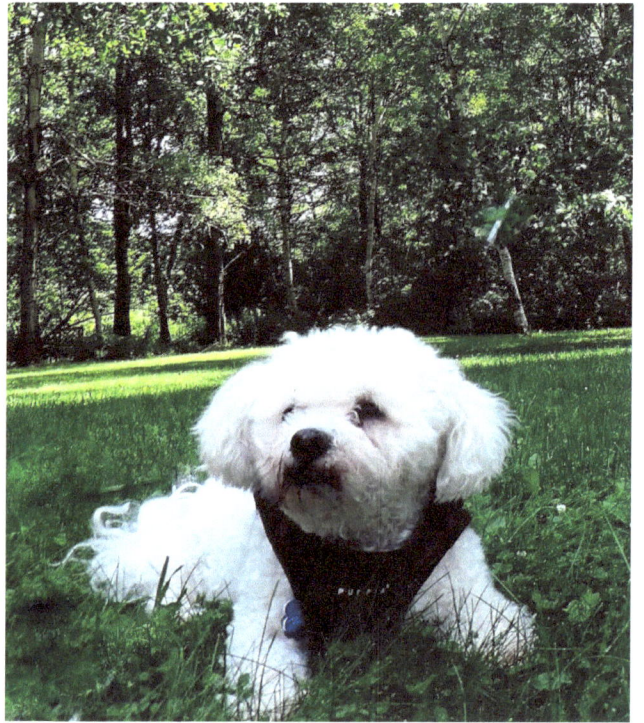

I watch while I lay in the grass.

I try to watch from the parents' computer but I still don't see anything that will answer my questions.

This is a mystery. What is it? It is really big and shaped like an elephant. But it doesn't smell like an elephant! It smells like a stick but is too big to be a stick!

And what is the other one behind the big one? It too smells like a stick but can't be a stick.

And why did my parents bring me here? They never stop for sticks. Are they telling me this is important? They are smiling at these sticks. Why?

This is a mystery too. My friend Gee put a bright flash in my face and stole my image and put it on human paper.

Then she put that near some flowers that smell great but look strange, but also look like something I should know. Why? What does it mean? It is a mystery.

These are the neighbors in my outside world.
This red bird sits on top of our bird seed treasure chest. She is serious. We don't mess with her.
This butterfly came to my house with his fifty brothers. I watched them wave their wings and then fly away.
This lady turtle laid more than 20 eggs up the hill from my pond. I saw her do it! I smelled them!
The two baby robins are waiting for their sister to come out from her egg. I found the nest on the porch and showed my mom!

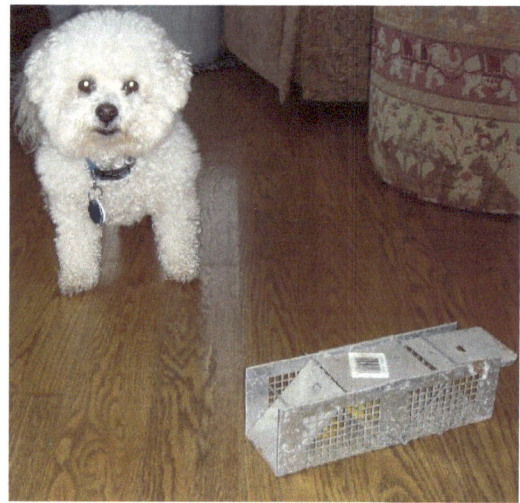

Chip also lives in my world. Chip causes a lot of problems.

Once chip had a party and stole and drank mom's peanut oil.

Look at his crazy hat. He lives in an underground house down that hole next to the hat.

Two times, Chip snuck into my house and I got him into this little box and put him outside the house again. It was my job to tell the parents when Chip got into the house. I was sleeping on the parents' bed when Chip jumped onto my father's arm. We were lucky that Mom had her tennis racquet!

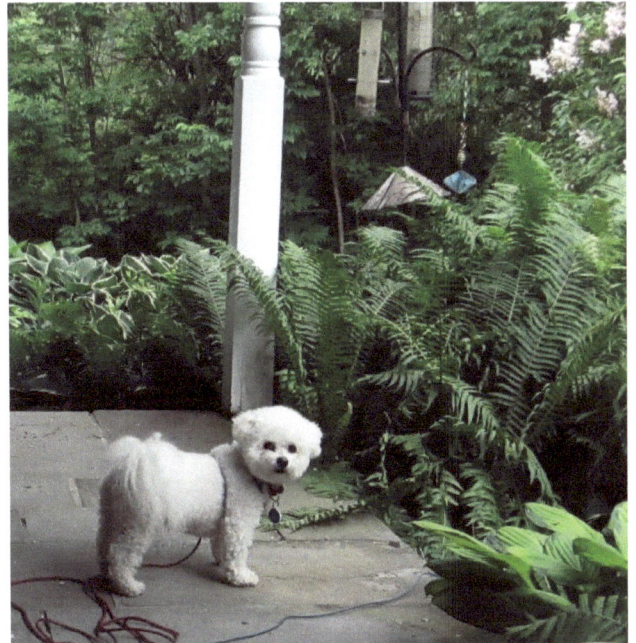

Some days my whole world is green and thrumming, and a thousand smells drift to me that say Alive! Alive!

On other days
my world turns
golden and the
smells turn musty
and deep. Nothing
is the same.
The gold season is
a mystery. What
happened?
Why?

What is this white cold fluff that falls through the sky?
Why does it come only in the white season after the
trees have given their leaves to the ground?
Why does it not come in the gold season or the green
season?
Why does it only come when the birds are gone and the
deer go hungry and run from men with guns?
Why?
What is this mystery?

Where are the smells? Where are the birds? Why is it so cold?
Why do my feet hurt without my boots?
Sometimes I just can't walk or I will disappear into the ground, so they
pull me on my blue sled.
Why do they put clothes on me? Where are the colors? What is
happening? Why?

All I want to do in the white season is this.
I am sure you understand why.
No mystery here.

What did this dog do to get turned to stone?

Why don't humans sleep normally?

What am I doing up here?
Why am I on the bottom shelf?

Sometimes they leave me home.
Alone.
Why? I do not understand!

Humans hunt lambs and bring one of
their legs home. Why they cook it, I just
don't know. Where they find the lamb is
a mystery. I never see lambs in the woods.

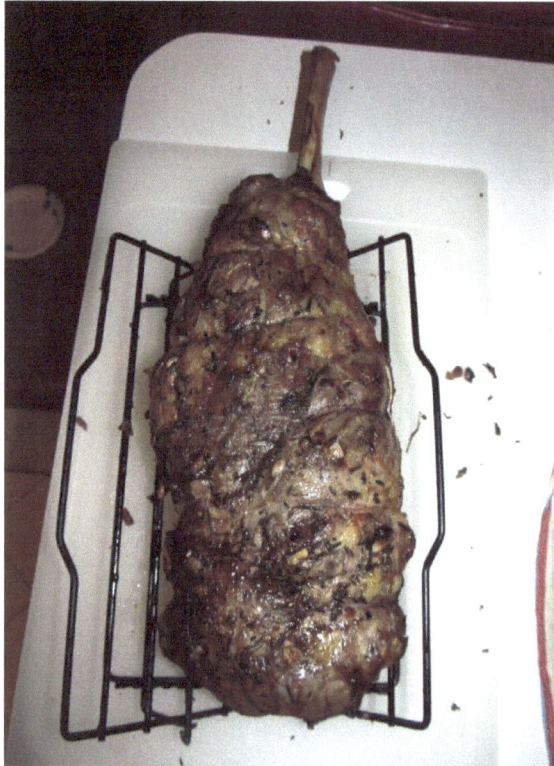

Before the cold white season, humans
hunt and cook these big birds. The sweet
smell fills the house for hours and drives me
crazy. Sometimes they do share it with me.

WITH BEEF CHUNKS
Trozos Con Carne de Res

GRAVY
TRAIN

This strange mixture is what they
give me to eat, everyday, day after day.
Why is my dish on the floor?
Why can't I eat at the table?
Why?

Humans sometimes roll small meat bites
into balls and then eat them. This is why dogs
chose humans to live with. This is very smart.
No dog would have ever thought of this!

Look at this spread. I love cheese. They will not give me any. All the relatives are here and they will not share. It is a mystery as to why these cheese gatherings occur.

Why is Riley in jail?

Why does this golden cloak
bring on the rain?

What kind of dog is this?

I like to stand under the swinging green thing and taste the black shroomy dirt underneath.

My mom said she would get me my own green thing but I cannot fit underneath it and there is no dirt to taste! Why?

My dad tries to explain to me what is going on and why things are like they are. I don't really know what he's talking about. But, he does smell really good. He smells like cookies and treats and ham sandwiches.

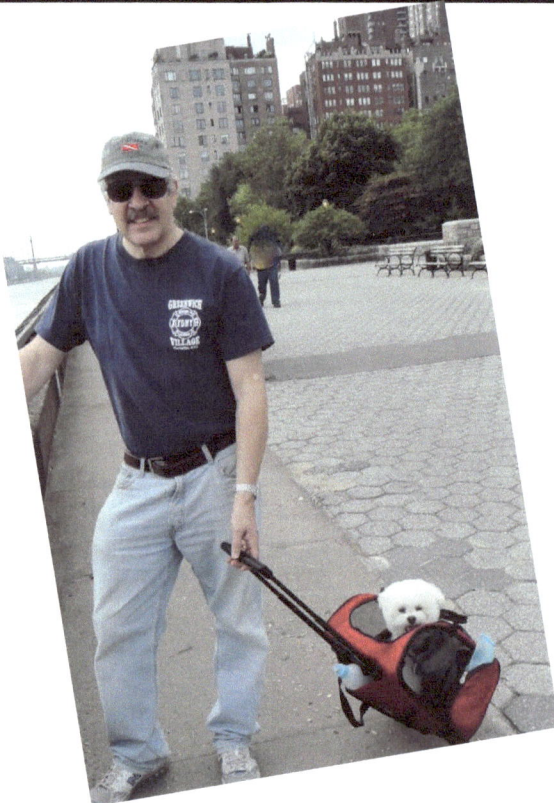

He takes me places. But if I walk too slow he pulls me in my chariot.

Other dogs don't know any more than I do. We are all curious but understand there will always be things we cannot understand. Humans make the rules and since we love being with humans and helping them, we just have to accept that there will be things of great mystery and unanswered questions.

Sometimes it can be very frustrating!

The world is such a wonderful place and even if we don't understand the mysteries, we should keep searching for answers.

Dogs know that loving our people, loving our life, and loving the world are the most important things we can do.

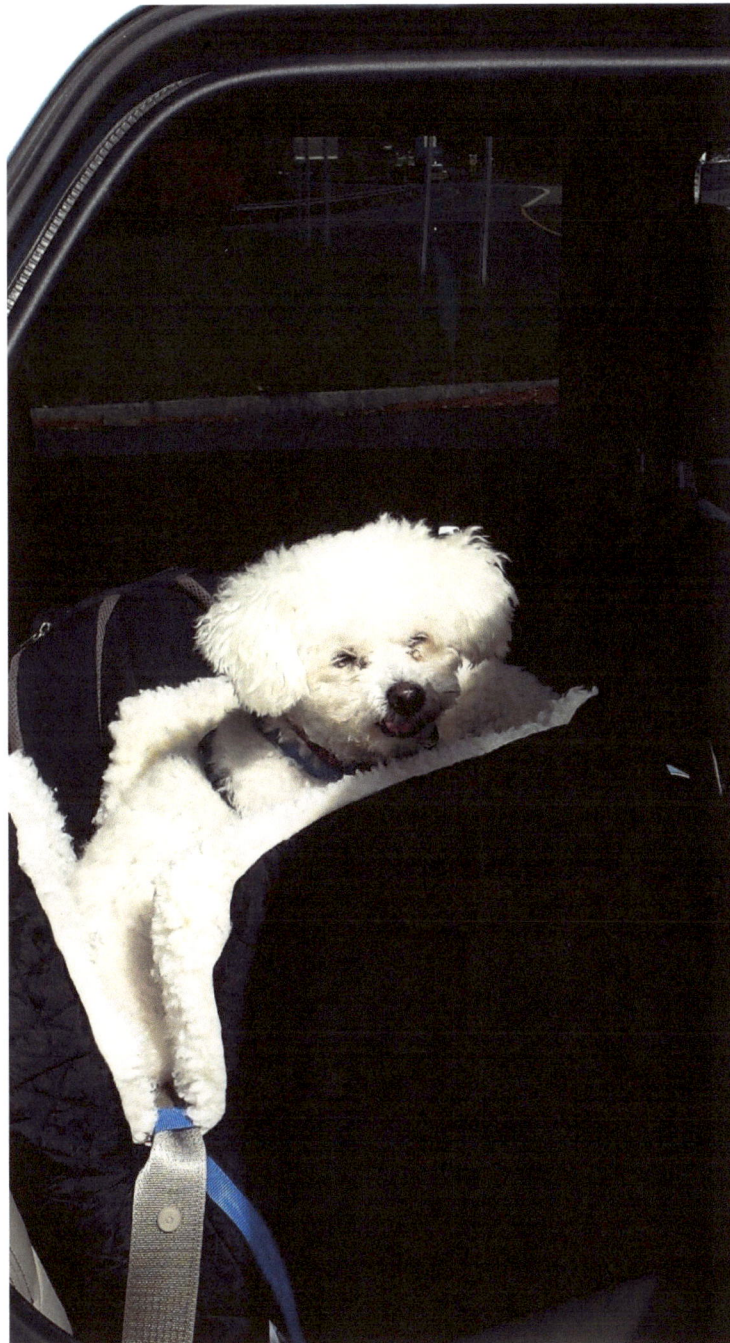

So make the most of today, it may be the best day ever!

About the Authors

My mom wrote all the words in this book for me as I cannot hold a pencil and have no computer of my own, but they are my words and my ideas. She also drives the car so we can go places and she cooks the bacon too. Sometimes she puts whipped cream on my food! I think she is my slave but I also think she is my hero. 🐾